fast

D1323728

ONE WEEK LOAN

PEARSON EDUCATION LIMITED

Head Office:
Edinburgh Gate
Harlow CM20 2JE
Tel: +44 (0)1279 623623
Fax: +44 (0)1279 431059

London Office:
128 Long Acre
London WC2E 9AN
Tel: +44 (0)20 7447 2000
Fax: +44 (0)20 7240 5771
Website: www.business-minds.com

First published in Great Britain in 2001

© Pearson Education Limited 2001

The right of Richard Templar to be identified as Author
of this Work has been asserted by him in accordance
with the Copyright, Designs and Patents Act 1988.

ISBN 0 273 65317 2

British Library Cataloguing in Publication Data
A CIP catalogue record for this book can be obtained from the British Library

10 9 8 7 6 5 4 3 2 1

Typeset by Pantek Arts Ltd, Maidstone, Kent.
Printed and bound in Great Britain by Ashford Colour Press, Hampshire.

The Publishers' policy is to use paper manufactured from sustainable forests.

fast
thinking:
budget

▶ **gather good information**

▶ **forecast effectively**

▶ **deliver your numbers**

by Richard Templar

contents

introduction

So, you found yourself having to do the departmental budget and you haven't got a clue where to start – and the clock is ticking. OK, let's be charitable and assume you're doing this budget because either you are newly promoted and this is the first time you've had the responsibility or your departmental manager is off sick with Wimbledon flu and you're stepping into the breach.

Whatever the background, you've put it off owing to pressure of work (see *Fast Thinking: Work Overload*) and the days have flown past and now the budget has to be done and on someone's desk first thing Monday morning. This only leaves you a couple of days.

So what are you going to do? Panic, of course. No, you're not. You are going to work through the stages easily and quickly following the guidelines in this book so the budget will be done – and done well – and duly on the right desk at the right time and in the right way.

Panic doesn't get the job done. Only by thinking at the speed of life can you accomplish all you need to. Trust me, you *can* do the impossible.

We all have too much to do, and let's face it budgets don't sound much fun, but with the help of this book you will come through not only on time and with your budget, but also with flying colours and looking cool. Here's how. This book will explain what is required of you: what a budget is and how it is put together; how to get the information you require; what you're supposed to do with the thing once you've done it; how to check it against reality; how to put it right if it all falls apart; and how to make sure you prepare better in the future (this means leaving more time). So let's get on with it.

It may well be better to leave more time in the future but all you are interested in is right now, right? You want the fast thinking version of budgets, which is:

 tips for putting together a budget that looks as if you know what you're doing

 shortcuts for producing the maximum while doing the minimum

checklists **to glance through to make sure you've got it all down on paper.**

... and all put together simply and clearly. And short enough to read, learn and inwardly digest, of course.

► work at the speed of life

This book is going to take you through the key stages of preparing, delivering and maintaining a budget – your budget, the one you've got to do *now*.

1 The very first thing you've got to do is establish the objective so you can understand how to prepare a budget – without a destination, the map is useless – your budget is the map, your objective is the destination.

2 Next, we have to know what sort of budget we are preparing – and there are all sorts from cash flow forecasts to profit and loss to distribution. And even the departmental budget varies enormously from company to company, and even from department to department.

3 After this comes the basic preparation – collecting the information, finding out how it was done last year, establishing what figures go where and why, adding on and subtracting to allow for growth and slump.

4 The next step is filling in the actual budget – entering figures into boxes and balancing it all out.

5 Then you'll need to know how to present it and to whom and how to justify it. And you'll need to know how to maintain it and keep up with the variances – those bits which differ from what you said they would be – so you get a lot of good use out of it.

6 Last of all, it's looking at what to do next time – when you've got more time – and all the speedy tips and hints you might like to file away ready for next year's budget – and the year after and so on. And we'll do the really fast budget: the budget in an evening and the budget in an hour.

fast thinking
gambles

So, don't panic. It's all in this book, everything you need to know – and no more. You don't need a long, rambling history of 20th-century economics or a lot of statistically pompous information about standards and variances. What you need is here, the minimalist guide to budgets for those of us who haven't got time to catch a breath let alone read waffle. You're thinking at the speed of life so you just want to get on with it.

Well, patience. First, you must be advised of some of the pitfalls before you can rush ahead. Let's face it, you've left this to the last minute either by choice or foolishness or accident and in an ideal world you would have a lot more time. But you haven't so you have to work with what you've got. The downside is that:

- ▶ The people whose help you need to prepare this budget may be reluctant to provide vital data at such short notice or may find it physically impossible.

- ▶ You may not be able to get hold of a copy of a previous budget this quickly, and without knowing what the 'house style' is you can waste a lot of time and effort.

- ▶ You don't have the time to check all your figures as accurately as you might have wanted to – this can lead to mistakes creeping in unnoticed.

- ▶ You may be tempted to take shortcuts and put in more assumptions than would otherwise be advisable – data are facts, assumptions are exactly that.

- ▶ You may be tempted to lump together a lot of items in the hope that no one will ask you to justify a final figure. Forget it. If you are shaky on some aspect then that's the area you will be asked about – it's an irony of life and there is no escape.

- ▶ You might be tempted by the urgency of this project to take other people's data at face value – don't. They may have their own mission, one of throwing you off course for their own ends. You need time to be vigilant, and check everything.

This fast thinking guide will get you out of trouble this time and have you coming up smelling of roses – but for next time allow longer, prepare better and enjoy the journey more. Now let's do it.

1 your objective

Faced with panic we all want to do something, anything. Well, you can't. Just do nothing for a moment or two. No panic. No activity at all. Except close your eyes for a moment and think about your objective. There, that's easy isn't it? Yep. Your objective is to get this darned thing filled in, on the boss's desk first thing Monday morning and save your job, bacon and reputation. Fine. There, that *was* easy. Trouble is that isn't your objective at all. First, you have to take a brief look at what a budget does.

DRAWING THE MAP

Apart from being a part of your job, what is a budget? It's a map. A map of the future. It might well be a treasure map of the future if used well. It tells you what is going to happen to your department over the next 12 months within the confines, obviously, of the fact that you cannot see into the future. But you can make reasonable guesstimates.

You can make assumptions based on sound managerial experience. You can use past form to produce a theory of what is going to happen. Then you can be on top of any events because you have predicted them:

- No more panicking because staff are off on holidays and you have no cover – you will have budgeted for that.

- No more frenzied terror when summer sales slump because you produce umbrellas and there is no demand in August for them – you will have budgeted for that and be expecting it.

- No more waking up at night in a sweat because there's no money left in your budget and you still have to pay for the Christmas party – you will have budgeted for that.

YOUR OBJECTIVE

So a budget is a map of the future – accurately and well defined and beautifully put together. It sings with perfection and you have orchestrated it with all the dedication and skill of a composer *par excellence*. But what is your objective? First you have to identify the objective and be very specific. It's no good saying: 'My budget is a plan of what is going to happen in my department over the next 12 months.'

That covers pretty well everything but what about the sales conference? Is that in there? Good, it should be. And the cost of paper clips? A new photocopier? Extra staff for the Christmas rush? Good. So you can refine your objective some more: 'My budget is a realistic plan of the next 12 months expressed in quantitative terms of what is going to happen to the finances of my department.'

That's better. It is a plan. Write it down.

REALISING YOUR BUDGET

When you compile a budget it has to be realistic or there is simply no point doing it. Your budget has to be attainable and realistic, and you have to be committed to it. If you set a target of selling 1,000 widgets a month then you have to move heaven and earth to achieve that goal. If you know in your heart of hearts you can only shift 600 then there is no point planning to sell more. If you also know that with a bit more effort and motivation you are going to move nearer 1,400 then say so in your budget. Use your budget as a tool for, not a hindrance to, good management.

INSPIRATION AND MOTIVATION

Under-budgeting is as bad as over-budgeting. It's your plan and it has to both inspire you and motivate you – and all your staff, of course, with whose help you will compile this budget. Without them you can do nothing (see Chapter 3 but not at

GOOD MAP READING

Set a destination you know you can get to but still have to strive for. Commit yourself to your budget and make sure you achieve it.

the moment as you are busy finding out about what a budget is).

Under- or over-budgeting is a bit like setting out to arrive in Birmingham and settling for Stoke – near enough you think, and quite similar. It's like crossing out Birmingham on your map and writing in Stoke. You ain't fooling anyone. The perfect budget is one which is realistic and achieved.

A FEW RULES

OK, so you've got an objective. You also need to be realistic and aim for the truth. Technically, there is nothing difficult about preparing a budget. There are a few rules and as long as you stick to them you can be successful. If, however, you go that little bit further you can produce not only an effective budget but also a really useful tool that will make you look good, be sharper and stay on top of your job better. Interested? Here's how.

Use your budget as a tool for, not a hindrance to, good management

Under-budgeting is as bad as over-budgeting

Making it manageable

Budgets can cover any period. Let's say yours is for the next financial year. Break that down into manageable chunks. It's pretty useless to have a budget which just gives a year's expenditure and a year's income. If you have a bad month (or a good one) there is no way of knowing. Thus you cannot make any adjustments to staffing levels or production or take any action based on the new information.

Break your budget down into the smallest time periods which actually mean something to you. It will probably be months but may even be weeks. A daily target is probably unrealistic. So let's assume you will break your budget down into 12 months. That makes it easy to handle, easy to see what's happening and easy to take evasive action should you need to.

Noticing where the money goes

So you've looked at the objective and you've decided on what sort of budget is required – this may well be dictated to you by a regional director or a senior manager and you have no choice in it – and next you will see how you can gather all the information needed. Relax. You are already a long way towards reaching your goal. Now, take a quick mental walk through your department and see it with a financial eye. Try to notice:

CHECKING THE DETAIL

Don't accept that a bottom line figure agreeing with what is budgeted is enough – you might be under in one area and over in another and these two are cancelling each other out. Someone, somewhere will spot this and you will be caught out.

▶ **what costs money**

▶ **where money is spent**

▶ **what staff you have and need**

▶ **what furniture and equipment you have and need.**

This shouldn't take long – now you can have a break.

for next time

Always allow yourself peace and quiet to think seriously about your objective. Be aware that your budget is one of your most effective management tools and try to put aside lots of time to work on it. No more leaving it to the last minute and having to panic. Be determined to be realistic and truthful in your budget and be committed to coming in exactly on budget – over and under are as bad as each other. Next time you will have this budget to follow on from so your job should be a whole lot easier.

Break your budget down into the smallest time periods which actually mean something to you

2 types of budget

You still have a lot of work to do and the clock is ticking those precious seconds away.

TYPES OF BUDGET

Now what sort of budget are you going to prepare? You might think there's only the one but there are several sorts of budget:

- ▶ sales
- ▶ production
- ▶ stocks
- ▶ capital expenditure
- ▶ cash flow
- ▶ profit and loss (including balance sheet)
- ▶ purchasing
- ▶ credit control.

Of course, all of these can be incorporated in one form or another into what is called a 'control budget' – a sort of master budget that covers everything. You have to determine which aspects of your department fit into your budget. Obviously if you are in the service industry you may not have sales as such or production. You don't make or sell anything. But you still need staffing costs, cash flow, credit control and capital expenditure. Or perhaps you only make and sell things, in which case a sales and production budget combined with profit and loss is your baby.

A *WHAT* BUDGET?

Let's briefly run through these different types of budget so we all know what we are talking about.

Sales

Simple really. A sales budget is exactly that – how much or how many are you going to sell? This may be broken down into distinct types of sales:

- ▶ **credit sales**
- ▶ **cash sales**
- ▶ **sold items – i.e. $1\frac{1}{4}$" widgets, $2\frac{3}{4}$" widgets etc.**
- ▶ **delivered items/collected items**
- ▶ **trade sales/public sales.**

Obviously if you are involved with sales you will know what sort of sales you make and thus what sort of costs you will have to budget for, such as:

- **sales staff**
- **delivery staff**
- **buying in stock**
- **overheads**
- **general running costs.**

Production

Again, simple when you think about it. Production is exactly that. Perhaps you are the manager of a production department, in which case your budget is all about how many of things you make. Your budget will stipulate how many each month set off against what it is going to cost you to make them.

Stocks

A stock control budget is one which deals with how much of anything you are keeping on the premises. Perhaps your business is very affected by seasonal changes. In this case a stock budget is essential. It's no good having money tied up in stocks of umbrellas over the summer months when trade is slack if that money would be better off invested in the high-interest account.

Capital expenditure

You need to budget for buying big things that your business needs. Perhaps that old photocopier in your department is going to need replacing sometime in the next 12 months – when are you going to buy it? Where is the money coming from? These things have to be budgeted for or events will have a nasty habit of sneaking up on you unannounced.

Cash flow

Perhaps your department needs more money at certain times of year than others – your cash flow budget will determine these slack times or over-rich times and allow you to make decisions and plan effectively.

Profit and loss (including balance sheet)

Suppose you buy in a second-hand car at £500 and spend £50 getting it through an MOT and another £25 on a new set of seat covers. And then you sell it for £600. You have made a profit of some £25. Brilliant. Now take out the cost of your time and the tank of petrol you put in and you will see what you actually made. Oh, so you cost yourself at £100 a day and the petrol was a fiver. Made a profit or loss?

A stock control budget is one which deals with how much of anything you are keeping on the premises

But suppose your department plans to buy ten cars a month and sell them; then you need a profit and loss budget to make sure that you aren't unexpectedly making a loss without realising it – or planning it. The balance sheet is a statement of where the business is at any one time – a sort of Polaroid snapshot.

Purchasing

If you are the manager of the purchasing department then you need a purchasing budget. This is concerned with buying stuff in and allocating which months you need more or less in – simple.

Credit control

If you are the manager of the credit department then you need a credit control budget which will tell you when you need more money or less, how to dish it out or call it in, and what to do with it once you've got it.

Sorry about the brevity of these budget explanations, but we really haven't the time to go into them in great detail. This isn't a textbook of budgets but a fast thinking guide to helping you with your budget – today.

DIFFERENT BUDGET TYPES

All budgets are different. The format varies a lot. Don't get into thinking budgets must always look the same – they don't. They vary from organisation to organisation. Smart managers know how to be flexible and think on their feet.

YOUR BUDGET

In your budget some or all of these examples may appear – but equally they may not. In an ideal world you will only be concerned with a simple budget which deals with what you spend, your staffing costs and your overheads. This may be set against some form of income or you may well be allocated an expenditure for the year.

Negotiating your budget

What happens is you tell the manager above you what you need in terms of finances for the year and they give you this amount or less. If you are good with your budget and prove a couple of things, you'll be a smart cookie and they will trust you and give you what you say you need. If you are sloppy and prove yourself unable to manage or are deliberately over-estimating some costs so you

Things have to be budgeted for or events will have a nasty habit of sneaking up on you unannounced

have a little slack to play with then they will pare you down accordingly. So:

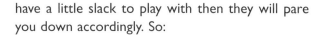 If you need six staff members, say so and budget for six – don't say seven and hope to have some money left in your budget to play with.

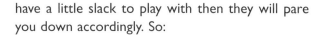 Check your budget every month (or more frequently if necessary) so variances can be dealt with quickly and decisively – a variance is a difference between what you said would happen and what has actually happened.

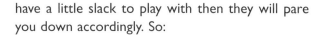 Be realistic when you budget and be truthful.

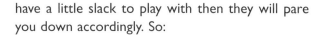 Don't make too many assumptions – data are facts, assumptions are guesses (OK, they may well be based on experience but they are still guesses); an assumption built on another assumption will always go wrong.

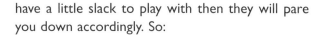 Update your budget and stay on top of it – information is only valuable if you use it.

A QUICK EXAMPLE

If this is the first departmental budget you've ever had to prepare, you may feel daunted by what it actually is supposed to look like. So, let's look at an example.

A simplified version

This is obviously a very simplified version. The column for this year would be broken down into 12 – one for every month – and some of the costs might well be broken down again, such as staffing

	Last year	This year	Variance +/−
Staff costs			
Travel			
Stationery			
Capital expenditure			
Furniture and equipment			
Heat/light			
Overheads			
Maintenance/repairs			
Petty cash			
Telephone costs			
Refreshments			
Totals			

costs, which may be broken down into full- and part-time or service staff and sales staff. Only you know what is required in your department.

Fleshing it out

OK, a quick rundown of each area in your budget. Your departmental budget may look nothing like this example – so learn to think laterally and put whatever you need into the boxes to compile your budget.

A variance is a difference between what you said would happen and what has actually happened

UNDERSTANDING A BUDGET

Look at the bottom line. The expression means exactly what is required of you. Don't get bogged down in detail – look at the very last line, the 'totals' line, and that will give you a pretty good overview of a budget.

Staff costs

These are what they say – how many people you have and what it costs to employ them including:

- **wages**
- **cars**
- **national Insurance**
- **private medical insurance**
- **pension contributions**
- **perks**
- **expense accounts**
- **clothing.**

Ask yourself: am I going to need more or fewer staff this year? Will I be recruiting or downsizing? Is there anyone to be made redundant? Do I need extra cover at any particular time of year?

Travel

These costs may include any of the following:

- ▶ **train tickets**
- ▶ **petrol**
- ▶ **first-class plane tickets**
- ▶ **bus fares.**

Ask yourself: do my staff move around at all and if so what does it cost me and is it a seasonal or varying cost that changes depending on the time of year?

Stationery

Obvious really. What paper do you use and how much? Postage stamps? Put them in as well and:

- ▶ **envelopes**
- ▶ **computer consumables (they may go here or in another section)**
- ▶ **pads**
- ▶ **invoices**
- ▶ **pens**
- ▶ **paper clips**
- ▶ **sticky tape**
- ▶ **post-it notes.**

Ask yourself: are my paper needs going to change through the year? Are there brochures to be printed? Do I have mail shots to be done? Can I economise anywhere here?

Capital expenditure

This may make accountants do a double take. It doesn't really go here according to them but we are talking budgets in general and learning not to get hung up on where things go – merely that they have to be budgeted for. Your own house style of budgets will tell you exactly where it all goes. You will have to work with your own house style even if you dislike it or it looks as if it was designed by monkeys. So, capital expenditure – big stuff, machinery, plant, not stuff consumed but stuff becoming part of the business.

Ask yourself: what big things am I going to need to buy this year? What needs replacing? Has everything been realistically valued?

Furniture and equipment

This might be chairs, or it could be computers. Again, it depends on your house style and what the finance department stipulates should go in here. (We'll talk about how you talk to them in the next chapter.)

Ask yourself: what furniture will need upgrading this year? What equipment is going to need replacing?

Heat and light

You've got to be able to see at work and be warm. It all costs money. Where's it coming from? Out of your budget, of course. Perhaps you may not even have to think about these as they may be taken care of as part of a control budget fixed by head office. But it doesn't hurt to know what they cost and how much you consume of them.

Ask yourself: what are my heat and light running costs? What do we spend the money on? Can we economise in any area here?

Overheads

These are sometimes known as fixed costs. They include the rent on the building or mortgages, leases on machinery, ground rents, that sort of thing. You may well have no control over them. They may not even be included in your budget or they may be allocated to your budget as a fixed percentage of their overall cost. Head office may dictate to you that you have to include such and such a figure for overheads without your even knowing how they arrived at the figure. It all varies.

Ask yourself: even if I have no control over them, do I know what everything costs? Do I have a full breakdown of the figures from the finance department?

Maintenance and repairs

Things go wrong. Things have to be fixed. Someone, somewhere has to pay for it and you have to budget for it. You may well wonder how on earth you are expected to know what is going to break and how much it is going to cost to fix it. You aren't; you budget a certain amount as a sort of reserve. At the end of the year you will know how close you were and what to include in next year's budget.

Ask yourself: have I anticipated everything and anything that could get broken, fall apart, cease working, become out of date?

Petty cash

Some departments don't have this any more. Some do. It's a small amount of money kept for buying things such as the odd bottle of milk when you run out. Whose job was it to budget for the milk? Who got it wrong? But you may have to budget a bit for very small emergencies.

Telephone costs

Calls and phones all have to be paid for. If you need an extra line put in, it has to come out of your budget. Catch the staff phoning their relatives in Australia during the lunch break? Well, it's coming out of your budget. And, no, you can't budget for your own private calls. Email calls may well go in here as well so don't overlook them.

Ask yourself: have I explored every aspect of telephone costs? Do I get charged a percentage for general switchboard finances?

Refreshments

Could be anything from the office coffee (which in some departments would come out of petty cash) to entertaining clients. Mind you, entertaining clients may come out of your travel budget if you go out to eat. You see what I mean about not getting bogged down about where it all goes until you actually come to fill it in? By then you should know, as you will have a copy of last year's. And you'll be armed with a lot of information about all this stuff – next chapter, wait for it.

Ask yourself: are there any categories of spending not covered in these examples? Have I missed anything?

Ask yourself: even if I have no control over them, do I know what everything costs?

for next time

Make sure you have fully and completely explored every avenue and aspect of your departmental finances. Make sure you know where money is spent and what everything costs.

Make sure you understand the house style – and if it sucks try to get it changed to a better style or a more usable one.

3 gathering information

Let's just take a moment to recap before plunging ahead:

- Your budget is a financial statement of what you expect to happen within your department over the next 12 months.

- It is no better to be below budget than it is to be above it.

- Budgets vary from organisation to organisation and it is better to know about budgets in general than to become bogged down with how your lot do it – you need to learn to be flexible in your thinking.

- Don't make too many assumptions when you come to fill in the detail of your budget.

- Be realistic and truthful.

- Any budget you do, you are going to have to justify and live with.

- A budget is very simple – you get a sum of money either allocated to you or from sales and you have to run your department financially by spending that money to ensure an efficient and successful office.

So let's see what we have left to do. First thing first: last year's budget. Unless you really are taking over a very new department there will be an old budget from last year. A good manager will have had this on their desk all year to check it against *variances* – a difference between what was expected to happen and what really happened financially – and to provide valuable financial information about the successful running of their department. So perhaps you are just taking over, filling a breach, stepping into someone else's shoes for a while or newly promoted. I'm sure you can be forgiven for not having last year's budget already to hand.

OK, so priority now must be given to getting hold of a copy. Whose shoes have you stepped into? Are they around to ask? Is their office still intact and their desk worth raiding? Does the finance department have a copy? Does your boss

thinking smart

A VALUABLE TOOL

A good manager never lets the current budget out of their sight for a moment. It is the most valuable tool in departmental managing. Without the budget you are lost at sea with no charts and thus no way of getting to where you are supposed to be.

It is no better to be below budget than it is to be above it have a copy? It doesn't hurt to ask these people. It doesn't hurt to admit you haven't got a copy. It doesn't hurt to be seen to be efficient and doing your job properly. No one can really compile a budget (unless it really is a brand new department) without knowing what has gone on before. So get it now before you do anything else. Off you go.

Got it? Good. Now you can begin to take it apart.

Ask yourself the following questions as you examine last year's budget very carefully:

- **Who compiled this budget?**
- **How accurate was it?**
- **Can I do better?**
- **Where are the biggest variances?**
- **What can I do about adjusting them?**

Now go through it again and check that:

- **there is nothing there that is now obsolete or irrelevant**
- **there is nothing there that is missing from this year's figures.**

Follow-ons and zeros

There are two ways of doing a budget – following on from last year's or starting afresh. Following on is known as a *follow-on* budget – see, this stuff is simple – and a new budget not based on last year's figures is known as a *nil* or *zero* budget. And obviously there are two reasons for this:

- 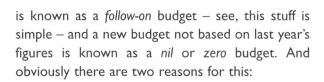 a follow-on budget where you use the same categories and merely update the figures makes your job a lot easier, but

- it may contain data that are now irrelevant or misleading, subject to the changes your department has gone through in the last 12 months. And a brand new budget may be much more accurate – and thus make you look better as a manager.

So, what have we got – last year's budget? Does it have figures from the previous year all neatly totalled up so you can see a sort of running history? Or does it look as if it was prepared only last year? Whichever one it is, you have to decide what sort you are going to do this time. If you are really pushed for time then a follow-on budget is quicker. You merely have to update the figures but be careful that you don't miss a new expenditure or include one that is now irrelevant.

But what if I haven't got last year's budget?

Then you'll need last year's accounts – which you should have anyway to compare to the budget. If you've got the accounts, you can use them in the same way you would the budget. And if you haven't got the budget or last year's accounts, you'll have to wing it. Go round the department and find out what money is spent on. But no one in their right mind would ask you to compile a budget with nothing to go on – it is unrealistic, unfair and just plain stupid.

Asking the right people

Now you need to ask some important questions of your last year's budget assuming you've got it:

▶ **How much money was your department given – what did it earn – last year?**

▶ **How many staff did you have and how many do you now need?**

▶ **What is the cost of those staff?**

thinkingfast

ADDING ON 15%

If you want to see what this year's budget *might* look like – not what it *will* look like or what it *should* look like – merely add 15% on to last year's figures. This won't give you an accurate budget or even one that is workable – but it will give you a budget and if you are really pushed for time, at least you will have a piece of paper with some figures on it. Then when you've got a bit more time you can redo it properly.

▶ **What, apart from staff, is the single biggest expenditure you need to make over the coming year?**

Some of these answers you may well get from the budget itself or from your knowledge of the department. Some you may need to get from another source – the finance department (that's right, you got it in one). Now how are you going to approach them? You could just pick up the phone and demand the information – but that would be a mistake. Get up from your desk armed with the questions you want answered and make the journey in person. Face to face is so much harder to turn down.

So, off to the finance department and politely enquire if it would be possible for them to give you the information you need. Words such as *favour* and *grateful* should tumble forth from your lips with such an enquiry, as should such phrases as *I know you're frightfully busy* and *I'm sorry to disturb you*.

thinkingfast

ASK POLITELY

If you want information from someone to help you complete your budget then go in person and ask humbly, ask nicely, say please and thank you and make it clear that you are asking a favour rather than demanding.

Get up from your desk armed with the questions you want answered and make the journey in person

Also be aware that other departments are compiling their budgets as well as you. They, too, may have recently asked for such information and the poor finance department might be overloaded with requests. Make sure yours stands out by being the politest or the most unusual – perhaps you could include a free round of drinks in the bar at lunchtime or a gift of some sort.

Have a ring round

And now that you are aware that other departments are compiling their budgets at the same time as you are it doesn't hurt to ring round the other managers and have a chat to see what problems they are experiencing or what information they may have access to that is unknown to you. Perhaps a new directive from head office limiting the amount of overtime worked has escaped your attention and you might be reminded of it. Or the fact that the new photocopier you wanted has just doubled in price and you didn't know – it pays to talk.

Now go back to your list of expenditure. Look at what costs you the most. This can be done, hopefully, while the finance department is on your case and is sorting out your staffing costs. What costs you the most? Is it computer consumables?

Stationery? Telephone calls? Whatever it is there is bound to be a person in your office in charge of it or monitoring it in some way. Make your way to their desk and get them to tell you all about it. Talk to your staff. The successful departmental budget is based on agreement and co-operation – not hierarchical dictate. Spend the next 20 minutes or so busily looking round at what costs you money – and talking to those who spend it for you. Ask for their advice, their views, their opinions. You don't have to include whatever they say but they may give you useful hints and tips that you might otherwise have overlooked.

Now you can have a break. You've sent out your runners to get information. You've talked to other departmental managers. You've talked to your staff. You've earned a break. But while you're having it you might need to know a few bits of useful information about collecting data for budgets.

Bear in mind that not everyone is as nice, as friendly or as co-operative as you are. They may have their own reasons for putting you on the wrong track. Always accept all information arriving in as useful but check its accuracy. Some people might not like to give you the information as quickly as you want purely because they want to see you fail or not be as successful as you'd like to

You don't have to include whatever they say but they may give you useful hints and tips that you might otherwise have overlooked

be. Always try to ask for information face to face as it's so much harder to be stabbed in the back when you are looking at the person. Always be polite and humble.

When you talk to your own staff bear in mind they may well have their own agenda and be asking for more than they actually need. This might be to make their job easier or to come in under budget (which they may think is a good thing, but which you now know is a bad thing).

Bear in mind that some staff will always ask for the impossible and others for the absurd. Nod and smile as if you are taking it all in and then go away and do your own thing.

How well do you know your boss?

OK, so you have marshalled your information. You've gathered some useful data and now you need to think about how you are going to present it and

thinking fast

ASK THE RIGHT PEOPLE

Try asking various people to gather information on expenditure for you. Whoever it is that monitors items of expenditure such as stationery should have a good idea of what it all costs and recent price changes.

KNOW YOUR OPPONENT

Your boss's job is to keep down expenditure. Your job is to run your department smoothly. These two may not be compatible. You need to know how to get your boss round to your way of thinking. You both need to be in a win-win situation. You can only do this by knowing your opponent, seeing them as a colleague and talking to them as a friend.

The successful departmental budget is based on agreement and co-operation – not hierarchical dictate

to whom. Remember it's not what you know but whom you know. How well do you know your boss?

Here are some questions to help you along the way:

- ▶ **Is your boss a stickler for detail?**
- ▶ **Do they see broad strokes rather than fine detail?**
- ▶ **Are they creative or accountancy-trained?**
- ▶ **How much leeway have you got for negotiation?**
- ▶ **Are they helpful or hindering?**
- ▶ **Are they part of the problem or part of the solution?**

Once you've got them pretty well tagged you can begin compiling the budget. You need to know how much detail to put in or collectively group. For instance, they may want details of every computer consumable listed separately under paper, laser cartridges, floppy disks and so on or they may only want a rounded figure for the whole lot. The first departmental budget I ever did was brilliant (at least I thought so) and the only question I got asked was, 'Where's the figure for light bulbs?' Yep, that sort of senior manager. If you know what your boss expects, you can save yourself either a lot of extra work for nothing or a lot of embarrassment and explaining later.

thinking fast

HAVE IT ALL TO HAND

Before you go into a budget meeting – and you will be called to one to explain all this – have all the information you need to hand and keep it all in neat, easy-to-read notes. This way when you are asked questions you don't need to shuffle through papers to see if you have the information – you will know you have it. And you won't be made to look a prat by having to say you'll look it up later.

I think we're about ready to start fleshing the whole thing out now so get a calculator and be ready to go.

thinking fast

Make sure you've asked the right people for the right information long in advance of when you need it to give them plenty of time to be as helpful and co-operative as you'd like them to be.

Make sure you've got a copy of last year's budget and check that it has been updated for any variances.

Make sure you know exactly what is expected of you and how much detail you are going to be asked to provide.

Always accept all information arriving in as useful but check its accuracy

4 filling it in

So, thus far we have worked out our objective, looked at the types of budget there are and gathered all the information we need, and now we are ready to fill it all in. Jacket off, sleeves rolled up and let's get on with it. But hang on, there are a few rules you should understand first:

- Don't use a budget as a weapon. It is a tool.

- Don't use it as an excuse to take on extra staff so you can cruise.

- Don't budget for resources you know you'll never need.

- Don't update last year's budget by simply adding on a set percentage to every figure unless you really are pushed for time – there may be a lot of changes to circumstances and this plan will come adrift very quickly.

- Don't set an 'easy' budget on the grounds you can say later that you've come in under budget.

- Don't pad a budget on the grounds that you think there may be cutbacks in subsequent years.

- Don't indulge in wishful thinking – be realistic at all times.

Don't set an 'easy' budget on the grounds you can say later that you've come in under budget

FIRST DRAFT

Get a piece of plain paper. You're going to do some work. Write down everything that you can think of that costs your department money. Look at last year's budget. What did you spend money on? What has changed since then? Do you spend more or less on each thing?

Write down these 'things' as a list and put a plus or minus by each of them if you think they have changed their priority. For instance, you may have had six staff last year and you know full well you are up to eight already this year. Then put a plus by staff costs – they've gone up. But what about transport? Maybe last year you all travelled a lot to meetings but this year you do most meetings by conference call. Put a minus sign by transport if you think it's come down. But remember you may need a plus by telephone costs to cover the increased usage by all those conference calls.

thinking smart

NOT JUST MONEY

The smart manager doesn't just budget for money but also for time and resources. A little time well spent with staff can have enormous benefits and should be budgeted for.

DON'T ASSUME

Don't assume last year's budget was correct. Keep thinking of what may have been missed off or included when it shouldn't have been. This is your chance to shine by pointing it out and putting it right.

Now you're getting somewhere. You should, by this time, have your staffing costs back from finance so you can begin to flesh this out. Once you've got your list of things that cost you money you can divide it up into things you have control over and things you don't. These are known as fixed and variable costs. Fixed costs are usually set by head office or your boss. Variable costs are the real ones

 thinking fast

USING THE SPREADSHEET

Remember your computer has a calculating function on spreadsheets – and use it. You can type a budget and use the calculating function to add up and insert figures into your document. If you are really good with spreadsheets, it can also keep running totals – thus if you alter one figure, it will automatically adjust all the other figures for you. This will save you time.

you can budget for as they are the ones you have some control over.

FIXED AND VARIABLE COSTS

Divide your expenditure into fixed and variable costs. The fixed costs are usually divvied up into 12 equal instalments so you can spread them over the 12-month period. The variable costs may not be. You have to look at all of them and decide if any or all of them are seasonal or subject to change for various reasons that would indicate you need to budget them differently during different times of the year. For instance, you might need more staff just before Christmas to cope with the rush. Or you need to budget for the extra brochures you always send out in the early spring. Or you know

thinking smart

HIDDEN COSTS

Whatever the item ask yourself what its concealed or secret cost is. The cost to you is not necessarily the cost that is visible. You may know that you pay a member of staff *x* amount as basic salary. But what about National Insurance (NI)? Sick pay? Holidays? Pensions? That's why it's so important to get on the right side of the finance department. You need them or you'll go badly awry.

you'll get an increase in costs in the autumn to cover the annual sales conference.

By now you should have a pretty good list of things both fixed and variable and with a note of any hidden costs as well as a plus or minus next to them to indicate their changes from last year. You can now fill in a year budget in rough. Draw out 12 columns (one for each month) and jot down in pencil what you think these costs will be in each area. You already know what sort of detail is required so you can lump things together if you can get away with it just so long as you can justify them if asked to do so.

There are a few other things to take into consideration as well.

STANDARDS OF PRECISION

Don't forget: 'We've all got to sing from the same hymn sheet.' The standards of precision are how much you are allowed to round figures up or down. For instance you might earn £56,000 a year (it's possible!) and with NI and pensions and car that might come out at £85,396.15. Is that the figure you are going to put into your budget? I hope not. It is too unwieldy. You need to round it up or down depending on the standards of precision allowed within your organisation. Staying up late calculating everything to the nearest penny is unproductive and not cost-effective. Let's say we round your salary up to £85,400. That's neater, simpler and understandable. Usual standards include:

- ▶ **Rounding pounds to the nearest hundreds – above 50 is 100; below 50 down to the lower hundred. For instance £57.95 would be £100, and so would £112.56.**

- ▶ **Rounding hundreds to the nearest thousand in a similar manner: £879.15 would become £1,000 and £2,391.22 would be £2,000.**

Find out what your industry standards are and use them.

RESOURCES AND USING THEM

Remember when you are compiling a budget that it is a social document as much as a financial one. It requires the help and co-operation of a large number of people to get it accurate and keep it sweet.

Here are the main resources and what you should use them for. Let's start with those nearest home:

People who work in your department

These are the people working directly under you and reporting to you. Use them for their experience and for bouncing ideas off. They may come up with things you'd never have thought of. They are also

You need to round up or down depending on the standards of precision allowed within your organisation

your colleagues and, as such, must be included in goal setting and agreeing their role in supporting you in fulfilling the departmental budget.

The boss

This is the one to go to for your goals and targets. They need to be sounded out for anything they're not saying as much as for what they are – what's their hidden agenda? And they will have one, believe me. You need to liaise with them, to support them and be part of the agreement process for your budget.

Your peers

Check these buddies out for how they are doing with *their* budgets – they may have information you don't – as well as offering support and encouragement (you're supposed to be a team, remember?) and getting them to buy their own copy of this book rather than borrowing yours. They may also have ideas and experience worth listening to.

The finance department

Tricky little devils these – and yes, I used to run a finance department so I know what it's like from the inside and what our (entirely justifiable) reputation is – so approach with caution and politeness. Once in get them to part with:

- payroll information
- accounts
- spreadsheet templates
- profit and loss information
- asset register (a list of everything the company or organisation owns with its value)
- accounting policies on key areas such as accruals and depreciation
- financial background to the organisation.

The personnel department

Usually slightly more approachable but still tricky. Be polite and charming and get them to part with:

- salary structures including pay grades and ranges
- details of bonus schemes
- details of pension contributions
- company policy on promotions and cost of living increases
- policy on employment levels.

Others

You would well be advised to check out the marketing department for sales reports and market trends as well as projections, and any sales

It requires the help and co-operation of a large number of people to get it accurate and keep it sweet

promotions that are being planned. And don't forget colleagues working for other organisations – they might identify information which you don't have that it might be useful to know in advance, such as changing industry standards. Keep abreast of your industry standards by reading the newspapers.

SETTING GOALS

Right back at the very beginning of this process we looked at setting an objective. You had to set one for your budget. How about getting your staff involved as well? You don't have to call it an objective – merely a goal. Set a goal for each person to do with collecting information or monitoring costs for this budget. That way you have lots of helpers all rooting for you and your budget. Get them involved and they will take care of your budget for you – then it's their baby too. Leave them in the dark – so-called mushroom management – and they will rip your budget to shreds just for the sheer fun of it. Get them to set goals for the people working under them – and so on. Then you have a sort of pyramid, an ant colony all working away keeping your budget in good shape.

PLANNING THE FINANCIAL CALENDAR

A year might be 12 months but those months are different lengths. February is a devil as it is so short whereas August is longer. You have to take these things into account. You also have to take into account bank holidays, Christmas, Easter, summer holidays and so on. You need a financial calendar which will show you when staff have to cover and be paid, but might actually be earning overtime or being paid at a higher rate such as double time or time and a half.

You need to be aware that each organisation has a different accounting period – the financial calendar. You might have a budget that covers 12 months or is divided up into four – one for each quarter. Or you might even have to operate one on a 52-week basis. Some seasonal businesses operate

thinking smart

ASKING IN ADVANCE

The smart manager doesn't wait to be asked to do a budget – they're already in there months in advance asking. Make sure you put your boss on the spot and ask for a budget package which should include last year's budget, a set of guidelines, a specific goal/objective of what is expected of you, a financial calendar, a description of the department along with an historical perspective, any expansion plans and a breakdown of staffing levels required. If you don't ask you won't get.

on two six-month periods. There is no right or wrong in any of this – they merely take into account differing needs. You need to know which your organisation uses – and use it yourself.

SECOND DRAFT

There. Now you can sit back and bask in the glow of a finished draft budget. Good. Now total it all up and be horrified at how much it is going to cost you to run your department. How does it compare with last year? A whole lot more? How are you going to justify it? How are you going to ask for so much? Well, you're not. This is your draft budget and as such will need to be slimmed down.

Shaping it up

First, you need to look at what areas you can trim money off. These will be the less prioritised areas that can be shaved without loss of efficiency or productivity. Take this first draft budget to the most senior person in your department whom you can trust and work well with. Show it to them. Ask them if they can see areas that can be slimmed down. After all, they are going to have to work with this as much as you are so their input is valuable. Ask them if they can see anything you might have missed. Even ten minutes doing this can

54

prove useful as often someone else will spot things you have overlooked.

Now back to your desk. By now you should have a pretty good idea of what you are doing and where you are going with it. Trim and trim and trim until you have shaved off every excess pound and every surplus ounce. The ideal budget is the one that is realistic and gets passed at the first budget meeting. There's not a lot of point putting in all this hard work only for it to be sent back again with the sort of 'good effort, now try again' note we all hate.

Having trimmed, total up the whole thing again. This time you should have a much more realistic figure to work with. Check the individual months' totals to make sure it all balances.

thinking smart

SEEING THE WHOLE PICTURE
The smart manager realises that their budget is only a tiny part of the whole picture. It is only a part of an overall budget strategy which is being built up department by department to cover the whole organisation. Once you see that your part is essential but only a part and not the entirety you accept changes to your budget more easily.

Now you have draft two it is time to really check the detail – and remember that too much detail will render your budget meaningless.

- **Look for costs which are non-essential. Maybe they are there from last year and are no longer really necessary.**

- **Have you identified all the hidden costs?**

- **Have you checked other people's figures for accuracy?**

- **Will this budget motivate your staff?**

- **Does this budget fulfil your objective?**

- **Have you been realistic and honest in all areas?**

Once you've answered these questions it's time for another quick cuppa and then on to preparing the third draft – the final budget.

Your budget should look something like the example shown if you've got it right. Let's suppose you are the departmental manager of the local fire department. You don't have any sales as such – merely call-outs – but you have staff, overheads and general running costs.

This is, of course, a very simplified version and yours may be much more complex but this will give you the general idea. You will notice some asterisks dotted throughout the budget. These will take the form of notes to make sure anyone else looking at your budget such as your senior fire chief will

Too much detail will render your budget meaningless

	Jan	Feb	Mar	Apr	May	Jun	Jul	Aug	Sep	Oct	Nov	Dec	Totals
Fixed costs													
Site rental	1000	1000	1000	1000	1000	1000	1000	1000	1000	1000	1000	1000	12000
Insurance	150	150	150	150	150	150	150	150	150	150	150	150	1800
Council tax	200	200	200	200	200	200	200	200	200	200	200	200	2400
Variable costs													
Staff	27000	27000	27000	27000	27000	27000	27000	27000	27000	27000	35000*	27000	332000
Heat/light**	4000	4000	3000	3000	2500	2500	2500	2500	3000	3000	3500	4000	37500
Staff meals	10000	10000	10000	10000	10000	10000	10000	10000	10000	10000	12500***	10000	122500
Maintenance	550	550	550	550	550	550	550	550	550	550	550	550	6600
Office admin	450	450	450	450	450	450	450	450	450	450	450	450	5400
Capital expenditure****	25000	25000	25000	25000	25000	25000	25000	25000	25000	25000	25000	25000	300000
Totals	68350	68350	67350	67350	66850	66850	66850	66850	67350	67350	78350	68350	820200 820200

understand and know what you are talking about – we will look at presenting your budget in the next chapter but for the moment you could add notes such as:

*   Increased staff costs in November to cover Bonfire Night
**   Heat and light costs adjusted throughout the year for seasonal variations – less heat and light in summer months
*** Higher staff meal costs in November to cover increase in staff
**** Capital expenditure budget for new fire appliance

Obviously, some or all of these will apply to you in some form or another. For instance, the capital expenditure may well not go in your departmental budget as it may be allocated elsewhere by head office or a senior manager, but this is the sort of thing you'd be expected to negotiate.

You will also notice the very bottom right-hand box. It has two totals which are – and must always be – identical. These are your monthly totals and your overall expenditure totals. They must always agree because if they don't you have got your sums wrong somewhere.

Now you know what you are spending every month and what on. What could be simpler? Or easier? Or faster? But time is passing and you still have to know what to do with this budget in the way of presentation and updating it regularly. If you haven't got time to read the next chapter in its entirety just read the bit about presentation – variances can wait until you come to do them, but I would recommend a quick glance just in case you get asked questions when you present your budget.

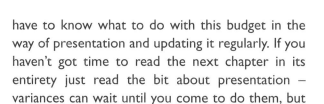

for next time

Be prepared for budget reviews. Yep, you gotta have 'em. Every now and again you will have to update your budget based on accurate accounting information flowing into your department. You have to keep on top of your budget and review it. You need to ask yourself if it still holds water or if it has all gone to pot. Ideally, you will do this over a cup of coffee with your boss in an atmosphere of calmness and mutual respect. I have, however, known no coffee, no respect and lots of shouting. If you are already prepared perhaps the shouting isn't necessary. Ask these questions of your budget before you are called in, to account for it.

▶ Is it consistent throughout?
▶ Is it accurate?
▶ Has it been trimmed to the bone?
▶ Does it have any data which you haven't checked?
▶ Are there assumptions based on assumptions?
▶ Can you talk through your budget without hesitation, repetition or deviation?

You are expected to answer: yes, yes, yes, no, no, yes.

Your monthly totals and your overall expenditure totals must always agree because if they don't you have got your sums wrong somewhere

5 updating the budget

THE FINAL FINISHED PROFESSIONAL BUDGET

Nearly there. Your budget just needs a few additions now to become a full and final budget. You need to add a couple of columns. After the final totals column on the right add another column and jot in it last year's figures. If you want to be really flash add two columns – one for the budgeted figure and one for the actual figure.

Now add another column alongside this and use a plus or minus symbol along with the percentage increase/decrease this year. So the whole thing should look a bit like the example (you may need to print it landscape to get it to fit on an A4 sheet).

There, now that's a professional budget. It includes figures for this year broken down into the 12 months and grouped according to whether they are fixed or variable. It includes figures for last year.

	Jan	Feb	Mar	Apr	May	Jun	Jul	Aug	Sep	Oct	Nov	Dec	Totals	Last year (actual)	Increase/ decrease
Fixed costs															
Site rental	1000	1000	1000	1000	1000	1000	1000	1000	1000	1000	1000	1000	12000	9000	+33.3%
Insurance	150	150	150	150	150	150	150	150	150	150	150	150	1800	1500	+20%
Council tax	200	200	200	200	200	200	200	200	200	200	200	200	2400	2200	+9.1%
Variable costs															
Staff	27000	27000	27000	27000	27000	27000	27000	27000	27000	27000	35000*	27000	332000	285000	+16.5%
Heat/light**	4000	4000	3000	3000	2500	2500	2500	2500	3000	3000	3500	4000	37500	36000	+4.16%
Staff meals	10000	10000	10000	10000	10000	10000	10000	10000	10000	10000	12500***	10000	122500	135000[1]	−9.25%
Maintenance	550	550	550	550	550	550	550	550	550	550	550	550	6600	6000	+10%
Office admin	450	450	450	450	450	450	450	450	450	450	450	450	5400	6700[2]	−19.40%
Capital expenditure****	25000	25000	25000	25000	25000	25000	25000	25000	25000	25000	25000	25000	300000	270000[3]	+11.11%
Totals	68350	68350	67350	67350	66850	66850	66850	66850	67350	67350	78350	68350	820200	751400	+9.16%

[1] Reduced food costs due to improved catering contract

[2] Reduced admin due to improved telephone contract

[3] Increase due to inflation / supplier's figures

11

CALCULATORS AND PERCENTAGES

There's a very simple way to work out your percentage increases or decreases over last year's budget. The simple way to do it is – take this year's figure. Take away from it last year's figure. Divide by last year's figure and hit the % button. There, that was easy. Let's work a quick example. Last year we budgeted for £1,200 for uniforms. This year's figure is £1,500. Thus 1,500 – 1,200 = 300 Divide by 1,200 and hit the % button = 25%.

You can also do this by taking this year's figure minus last year's figure, dividing by this year's figure and multiplying by 100 – same result.

Carry a calculator and be prepared to work out any percentage increase and look flash while doing it. Very good.

It has its percentage increases or decreases. It is all totalled and it balances. Put it on one side for the moment and let's have a look at how to present it.

BUDGET MAKEOVER

So, where are we going with this budget? We've set our objective, talked to our staff, gathered information, compiled and trimmed the thing – and now? Now we are going to turn it into the most professional-looking budget you've ever clapped eyes on. Yep, we're going to do a budget makeover that will make it so impressive you'll have it approved straight away and you'll look seriously cool.

When chancellors of the exchequer present a budget to the house they don't just hold up a sheet of paper with some impressive-looking figures on it. Oh, no, they talk it through by way of a speech. Relax, you don't have to make a speech. But what you do have to do is talk your budget through on paper.

Let's run through the exact stages:

- ▶ **Use A4 paper.**
- ▶ **First page should be a title page giving the name of your department, the year the budget covers and the word 'budget' (and your name, of course).**
- ▶ **Second page should be a contents page which is a clear listing of what the reader should expect to find in the following pages.**

thinking smart

A SLOPPY PRESENTATION CUTS NO ICE

A well-presented budget looks professional and looks as if you know what you are doing. If people are filled with confidence by your presentation they will transfer that confidence to your figures, your calculations and most importantly to your budgeted requests. A smart budget presentation gets more money for your department.

- Third page should be the actual budget – and no budget needs to stretch beyond one sheet of A4 paper, although you may need to print it landscape to get it all to fit – all neatly typed and looking very professional by now. Any notes will appear on the next page and you can link them with an asterisk or a footnote number [1].

- Fourth page should be your notes expanding on anything that might need explaining but try to keep these notes to a minimum and never more than one page.

- Fifth page is reserved for any subsequent information that needs clarity. In the budget example in the previous chapter we had a monthly figure for office admin. Let's suppose your boss wants to know exactly how that figure is arrived at. You could take the annual figure of £5,400 and break it down:

Office admin		5400	
Stationery	2200		
Computer consumables	1200		
Telephone	2000		
Total	5400		

---

[1] They look like this.

Thus page 5 is a sort of mini-budget that can run to several pages. You might need to do a mini-budget for staff costs, a breakdown of staff meals, a breakdown of heat and light costs (remember the light bulbs) or a mini-budget for maintenance. Label each page 5a, 5b, 5c and so on. Any explanatory notes for any page 5s can go at the bottom as footnotes rather than on a separate sheet.

Now present the whole thing in a nice plastic folder with a clear cover and you have a good-looking document which will get the job done.

Now you are nearly ready for that deadline tomorrow morning. You've done your budget and presented it professionally. Well done. If you've still got a bit of time in hand, read the next bit about variances and what to do about them.

VARIANCES AND WHAT TO DO ABOUT THEM

We all get them. They are nothing to be ashamed of. They can be treated. Variances are the differences between what you said would happen and what has actually happened. Suppose you budgeted £200 a month for maintenance and suddenly, in April, you have to spend nearly £1,000 getting a lift engineer in to sort out a particularly trying problem. Your budget may look like the following.

You have to talk your budget through on paper

Maintenance	Budgeted figure	Actual figure	% variation	Notes
January	200	197	1.5%	Normal month
February	200	210	(4.7%)	Had to repair coffee machine
March	200	145	37.93%	Nothing broke down so saved money
April	200	1000	80%	Lift broken down – engineer called out 3 times
Sub-total	800	1552	48.45%	Service contract being looked into
May	200			
June	200			
July	200			
August	200			
September	200			
October	200			
November	200			
December	200			

April's budget may be some 80 per cent over but your sub-total shows you are only 48 per cent above budget overall. So you've got the rest of the year to pull back and you are on top of the variance:

▶ **You know what happened.**

▶ **You know why it occurred.**

- ▶ **You are taking steps to make sure it doesn't happen again.**
- ▶ **Already you are negotiating with the lift company for a service contract.**

When questioned by your boss you can show you are on top of your job, you are efficient and you are ahead of the game. Well done. You are also noting down when you are under budget – which we know is just as bad – and you are demonstrating that you are aware of what is going on in your department.

Good. That's about it for today. Go home and enjoy a well-earned rest. You can be relaxed and even look forward to the morning knowing you have done a good job and pretty well tied up all the loose ends. There are a few more things you really should know before having to sit in a budget meeting but not for now. If you have time this evening, read the next chapter.

thinking smart

STAYING ON TOP OF VARIANCES

The smart manager gets the staff to report any expenditure that is above or below the normal. That way there are no surprises at the end of the year – you already know or can anticipate when your budget is wandering off course.

Make sure last year's budget has been updated for variances and all the columns are complete and balanced.

Make sure you understand percentages and what they can tell you about your department's finances.

Leave enough time to produce a really professional-looking budget neatly presented in its own folder with a clear plastic cover and no coffee stains. Get somebody to do it for you if you are pushed for time or if you are hopeless at this kind of thing.

Update your variances as you go through the year – it is all too easy to forget about them but a smart manager concentrates on them and stays ahead of the pack.

Take appropriate action to deal with any major variances before they get worse.

Update your variances as you go through the year – a smart manager concentrates on them and stays ahead of the pack

6 for next time

So you've got through the budget and produced a professional working document that you can be happy with – and so can your boss. Now you need to turn into a budget expert. You're going to have to present your budget tomorrow morning, and you will doubtless have to attend some sort of meeting where you will be questioned about your figures.

You don't have to do anything except read this chapter – make notes if you want to – but sit back and pay attention. Read slowly and carefully and if you don't understand anything read it again slowly until you do. There is nothing difficult here or complicated or even daunting. It is all easy stuff that may simply be new to you or unfamiliar territory.

WHY BUDGETS GO WRONG

It doesn't matter how hard you try or how on top of your job you are, bad things happen to us all. Just when you thought you were coming out spot on budget something terrible happens or a memo arrives from head office that throws your budget completely off track. This happens to us all and can't be helped. We have to live with it and get on with the job.

There are a few things we can do, however, to minimise the occurrence of bad things. Look again at your budget – mentally, you don't have to go and get it: what is your biggest cost? Bet it is staffing. It always is. People cost money – lots of it. And staff costs change. Staff costs change a lot and invariably these changes are outside your control. They can change for a variety of reasons:

- ▶ **Someone gets an increase in salary because they are promoted.**

- ▶ **There is an across-the-board increase to cover a cost of living rise.**

- ▶ **Someone gets an increase because the time they have served warrants a step up to the next salary level.**

- ▶ **Someone gets a bonus for good performance.**

Now you can see at a glance that some of these – if you are really on top of your job – could have been foreseen and budgeted for. Promotion, long service increases and bonuses are all expected. An across-the-board rise to cover inflation may not have been foreseen but you should have allowed for it as it probably happens nearly every year.

Being on top of your salary costs is the best thing you can concentrate on. Here are a few tips:

▶ **Very few organisations – or even departments – are up to their full quota of staff at any one time. Use the slack to counteract any rises in salaries you hadn't allowed for.**

▶ **Working out a *total* cost for an employee including all the hidden costs, such as National Insurance, takes a lot of time. How much better if you know the basic salary and then can add on a *payroll overhead percentage*. Easy to do if you know how. Here's how. Take the total cost of your payroll and take away the cost of basic salaries and overtime. Divide this figure by the cost of salaries and hit the % button. This gives you the payroll overhead percentage. Now you don't need to trouble the finance department too much as you are using the same calculation they will be.**

thinkingfast

KNOW YOUR PAYROLL OVERHEAD PERCENTAGE

You really should always know what percentage of your total expenditure your staff costs are. They contribute the biggest chunk of money and are worth staying on top of. This is where the bulk of your expenditure will be and you should know it off by heart.

- Don't let staffing levels creep up unnoticed – it's easy to do so. Whoever, within your department, is responsible for taking on new staff has to be made to justify each new employee individually. Make them answerable to you in blood if necessary but monitor your staff levels like a hawk. Staffing is the biggest single area where your budget will fall apart if you don't watch it.

- Watch out for temporary staff and emergency cover. These two areas can again turn your budget into so much wastepaper if you don't monitor them. Same goes for consultants. If they are called in, they have to be paid for – and it all comes out of your budget.

STAFF BUDGET

Yep, you need one. Even if your boss doesn't want one as a breakdown of staff costs in your main budget you certainly need one – and you need to refer to it a lot. No manager can keep track of their

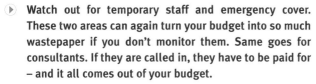

thinking smart

DONKEY WORK

Get your staff to do the donkey work for you – collecting information, checking key areas of the budget for variances and watching out for changes. Try offering an incentive bonus for various areas of the budget – 'Look, if we stay within budget for staff travel I'll take you all out for a slap-up meal at the end of the year' – that sort of thing.

Name	Position	Gross	NI	Pension	Benefits	Payroll cost	Notes
F Burrows	Department manager	60000	4638	9000	10000/car	83638	
T Bear	Assistant manager	40000	4380	6000	8000/car	58380	
W G Keldfelt	Section leader	30000	3120	4500	4000/car	41620	Due to retire in June/July
C Milton	Assistant sec leader	24000	2496	Nil	Nil	26496	Promotion July?
J Willis	Admin clerk	20000	2080	Nil	Nil	22080	Due pay rise in November for long service
R Jay	Apprentice	14000	924	Nil	Nil	14924	Qualifies Feb – pay rise to cover – need new apprentice
Totals		**188000**	**17638**	**19500**	**22000**	**247138**	**Payroll % 31.45**

USE WHAT YOU KNOW

We all think size matters. But does it? You may be persuaded to upgrade your computer programs constantly, including spreadsheets. The trouble with this is it all takes time to learn – and the bigger and newer you go the more glitches, gremlins and gobbledegook you are going to encounter. Stick with whatever package works best for you. Sometimes even ignoring the computer and working out your basic budget with a pen and paper can be quicker, simpler and easier to play around with.

finances without knowing their exact staffing requirements and the overall payroll costing.

Shown opposite is a simple example so you know what we are talking about.

There, that wasn't too difficult, was it? That's a payroll budget. You could break it down into months if you wanted or quarters or even six-monthly periods. Use whatever you need to be the smartest manager around.

BUDGETS FOR OTHER EXPENSES

Let's look at a few hints and tips to turn you from an ordinary manager into a really smart cookie – a supermanager of budgets.

KNOWING YOUR PERCENTAGES

The smart manager knows what each category in the budget costs as a percentage. Thus you might say, 'Oh, staff costs are 57% of my budget, heat and light 14%, maintenance 2.7% and admin costs 23%.' If you keep tabs on these percentages you will know what is going up or down, what is happening and why. You will look seriously flash and all you need is a calculator and a simple equation (total budget minus the individual cost, divided by the total budget, hit the % button and minus 100). Need an example? Of course you do.

Total budget is 820,200 less the staff costs of 332,000 = 488,200 divided by the total of 820,200. Hit the % button = 59.52 less 100 = 40.47%. Easy.

Another one? Total budget of 820,200 less staff meals of 122,500 = 697,700 divided by the total of 820,200. Hit the % button = 85.06 less 100 = 14.93%.

▸ **Remember not every month is the same length** – we will look at how you calculate a calendar budget in a little bit.

▸ **Irregular expenses.** Some things you pay for only once a year – perhaps a business licence – and you need to know in which month it is to be paid, so you can budget for it, and how much it will be. Or you could allocate $\frac{1}{12}$ per month.

▸ **Watch the seasonal expenses.** These could be gas or oil for heating. And watch for seasonal variations in price – oil is cheaper in the summer.

- Make sure you have a clearly defined policy for such things as travel expenses. This way your staff will know what they can spend in advance. For instance outlaw first-class travel or specify a price band for hotels – and don't let them get away with anything the first time or your budget will go haywire by the end of the year.

- A lot of expenses can be directly related to the number of staff. As staff levels rise so do your telephone costs, office supplies and travel. Set limits if it helps you keep costs down.

- Analyse your department's history so you know when money is being spent, why it is being spent and how it is being spent.

thinking fast

SETTING REALISTIC TARGETS

If your staff exceed your budget you need to know – and take action. But at what level do you step in and get heavy? You need to set a realistic level under which you are not bothered. For instance, if your stationery budget is £240 for the month and your senior admin person spends £245, does it warrant your being involved? The time taken to inform you and for you to choose either to take action or ignore it may cost you more than the amount by which the budget has been exceeded. Set a target of say 5% or 10% above or below and stick to that. Only if spending creeps beyond that do you need to be involved.

There. That will do for now. We need to look at some of the technical terms you might come up against during budget meetings. After all it doesn't help to feel you've been made to look small just because someone uses a technical expression that you don't understand.

BUDGET TERMINOLOGY MADE CLEAR

Every organisation uses different terminology, often to mean exactly the same thing. If you are new to the company it can be a bit daunting to have to ask what they mean. Here are a few terms to help you along:

- ▶ *Variable budget*. This is one of two things. First, it might well be where the budget figures are all expressed in percentages rather than pounds. Or it can be used to denote a budget that uses variances to provide running totals throughout the year – you use less so less gets transferred into next month's budget. Always ask 'Which sort of variable budget are you referring to?' This throws the onus back on to the enquirer and makes it look like you really know your budget stuff.

- ▶ *Historical trend budget*. Simple. This is a budget that uses last year's figures and merely updates them by a fixed percentage. It's quick but not very accurate.

- ▶ *Line itemised budget*. This is very similar to the examples we have used in this book: a simple budget that is basically a list of expenditure.

▷ *Fund budget*. This is a budget that allocates a large sum of money (a fund) to a department and then allows the department to spend it and allocate it later.

◀ for next time

Make sure you've got a budget package long before you need to sit down and do your budget. If your boss isn't too keen on giving you a package, ask why not and be assertive. You cannot be expected to do your job properly without the necessary tools. Keep your budget updated for variances and that way you won't be taken by surprise at the end of the year.

Monitor and monitor and monitor. Check every detail so you stay on top of it. Your budget is one of the most important tools you can have as a manager. If it is used properly, efficiently and well it turns you from an OK ordinary manager into a kick-boxing Ninja manager who inspires awe and admiration. All you need is a decent calculator and the knowledge given you in this book. Practise the simple equations until you know them off by heart and can work out your payroll percentage or what percentage a particular expense is within the total of your budget at the drop of a hat.

I know you can do it.

7 special budgets

So we have looked in some detail at your yearly departmental budget – and you've successfully completed it, handed it in, been praised for all your hard work and excellent presentation. So what's left? Well, there are times when you need a one-off budget – a special budget which might form a sub-part of your yearly budget or not. Suppose the MD calls you up and asks you to do a special three day exhibition to launch the new MX21. By now you know what your first question should be, don't you? That's right: 'what's my budget?'

Suppose the MD says you can spend ten grand – and not a single penny more – well, now you know what you've got to work with.

It might, of course, not be an exhibition. It might be:

▶ A conference
▶ A Royal visit

- A sales promotion
- A new product launch
- A PR event
- A trade show
- A commemorative lunch
- A retirement party
- An award ceremony
- A Christmas party
- A works outing

But back to the chase. It's no use just going to the trade exhibition and hoping that the ten grand will see you through. What if you run out of money after only one day? What you gonna do then? Pack up and go home, and tell the MD that you decided to prune the three days into one? I don't think so. Stuff would hit fans.

THE SPECIAL BUDGET

So what are you going to do? The special budget of course. And the first thing you need to do is plan the exhibition. Now that is outside the remit of this book (see *Fast Thinking: Project*) so come back when you've done that.

There are times when you need a one off budget – a special budget

Back already? Good. Now you know how many staff you'll need, what the stand is going to cost you, whether or not you need to put staff up in hotels, travel arrangements, sales material, refreshments, that sort of thing.

Now the interesting thing about a special budget is that there is always an overlap between it and your normal departmental budget, for instance staff costs. The staff you take with you – and yourself of course – are already budgeted for moneywise out of your regular departmental budget for salaries. But what if they work overtime? Is that to be taken out of your special budget or out of your departmental budget? Only you can decide but normally they would

thinking fast

PRINTED BUDGETS

When you start to work out your trial budgets, map out a table on your word processor and print out several copies. This saves time when you are filling them in, in rough. As you do each one and it is superseded by another you can throw the initial one away but you still have lots of blank tables printed to keep you going. Saves time and effort and makes your trial budgets a lot easier to work with.

receive their normal salary from departmental budget and the overtime payment from the special budget. But, and this is where things get complex and you have to think at the speed of life if you're not to come a cropper, the job they normally do back in the office ain't gonna get done while they're strutting their stuff on the exhibition stand.

So not only do you have to budget money, you also have to juggle people (no, don't even think about that). Who is going to replace them – and you – while this exhibition goes on? Do you need to get in replacement staff? Temps? Can you get existing staff to cover? Pull in someone from another department? Let it all go hang until you get back? You have to make that decision – and quickly if you're to get on with this budget (see *fast thinking: decision*). Once you know how you are allocating your staff you can move on to the really interesting stuff such as paying for the stand, getting in exhibitor organisers, hotels, travel, and refreshments of course.

You should now be ready to start a trial special budget which is basically a list of expenditure. You add it up, and hopefully you haven't forgotten anything, and it comes in at less than the £10,000 you were given to play with. It might look something like this:

Not only do you have to budget money you also have to juggle people

Staff costs for overtime	£3000
Exhibition stand rental for three days	£600
Sales material and printed matter	£500
Hotel accommodation	£4500
Staff meals/refreshments	£800
Travel	£240
Exhibition organiser	£6500
Total	£16140

Ah, we have a problem. You only have ten thousand pounds and already you've allocated over sixteen. This is why a special budget is so important. If you hadn't done this exercise, you would have overspent. That means you would have had to make up the shortfall out of your departmental budget which would have thrown that off track. OK, let's regroup and rethink. What can we cut down on?

SECOND DRAFT

Firstly look at your biggest expenditure – staff overtime, hotels and exhibition organisers. Which of these can you pare down?

BROADEN YOUR HORIZONS

If you like organising then this job is for you – the special budget. It makes life easier and faster if you know how to budget well and keep control of expenditure. You'll be more than likely to be offered the plum jobs organising special projects – this gets you out of the office and allows you the chance to shine and look good.

Staff costs and hotels go hand in hand so let's look at these two first. You need to pay the staff overtime, of course, as they will be working longer hours and away from home. But what if you sent them home at the end of the day instead of putting them up in expensive hotels where they will only run up colossal bar bills and probably get themselves into trouble? You need to find out if it is practical to send them home at the end of each day. How far away is the exhibition? Are there frequent trains? Can they drive there and back in reasonable time?

Are there cheaper hotels? What about a B&B? Do you need to pay them overtime or could you give them time off in lieu? If you don't know the answer to this one, go and ask them –

If you hadn't done this exercise you would have overspent

hypothetically, at this stage. What if you paid them an exhibition allowance and let them spend it in anyway they chose, then they could drive home if they wanted to or stay in whatever accommodation they preferred. They might even have friends in the area and stay somewhere for free – no, you can't ask for the allowance back if they do this. Let's suppose you choose to pay them an allowance and you set it at £400 per person per day. And you need three staff with you – forget about yourself for the moment – that would cost you £3600. Damn. Too much. Cut it down and pay them £200 per person per day – that's only £1800 – saving £1200 – good. This also cuts down on your overtime bill as you officially dispense with the staff once the exhibition closes at the end of the day rather than paying them for all the time they are away from home. Most exhibitions start earlier and go on later than normal office hours, but you are paying them this very generous exhibition allowance so you might get away with not paying them any overtime at all – if you are clever and present it to them in such a good light that they think you're doing them a favour. Let's suppose you sell it to them well and they accept. You've slashed your overtime to nothing and reduced the hotel bill to a mere allowance of £1800 – simply brilliant.

NEGOTIATING UPWARDS

Just as you can haggle with suppliers and the like, so you can negotiate with your boss. If they say they want you to organise a conference and your budget is five thousand and you know this to be a bit on the light side – then say so. And make sure you have enough evidence to back up your claim. Keep records of all special budgets you do so you can justify an increase. Quickly whip out your proof and you take the wind out of their sails and pull the rug from under their feet – so to speak. If you catch them on the hop, they'll be much more likely to grant an increase than if they have time to think about it.

NEGOTIATING COSTS

Now what about these exhibition organisers. Seems to me they are taking you for a ride. Go back and negotiate them down. I know that sounds easier said than done, but we are all in the market place and no one objects to a little haggling. Phone them up and question their quotation. Believe me most will drop their price a little if you query it, or suggest a slight amendment. Suppose you say that the quote seemed a bit steep and you'd like it for less as your budget doesn't allow for such a high price – good one that, always blame the budget and not yourself for querying a quote – for you next tactic, suggest

You are paying them this very generous exhibition allowance so you might get away with not paying them any overtime at all that you and your team will be responsible for clearing up afterwards instead of them and that you will provide staff to put out all the promotion material instead of them – obviously they have to be allowed to do their very professional job of putting the stand up, providing an impressive display, putting in the lighting and electrics and all that. Now they might well come back and agree a discount. Say they suggest £5700. You say 'make it five and a half and you've got a deal', chances are they will agree. You've now cut your exhibition organiser's budget by £1000 – again, brilliant. Let's have a quick look at a revised trial special budget:

Staff costs for overtime	Nil
Exhibition stand rental for three days	£600
Sales material and printed matter	£500
Hotel accommodation	Nil
Staff exhibition allowance	£1800
Staff meals/refreshments	£800
Travel	£240
Exhibition organiser	£5500
Total	£9440

OK, now we're getting somewhere. You've got a budget that falls below the ten grand you have to play with. Excellent. But you have forgotten one thing – yourself. What are you going to pay yourself for this exhibition? Strikes me you should pay yourself the same as your staff – the £200 per day – total of £600, I think. That takes you up above your target by £40 and you have no contingency to play with. A contingency is an emergency amount for emergencies – simple, huh?

LOOKING AT THE DETAIL

OK, let's now look at the lesser expenditure. You probably won't be able to negotiate the rental on the stand down so forget that. The cost of the sales

thfhkfhkfprmt thinking smart

11

ANTICIPATING THE SPECIAL BUDGET

Smart managers think on their feet. So if you hear that there is going to be a royal visit in six months time, then you know it's sod's law that you'll be given the job of organising the painting of the lavatories – or whatever is required. Stay one step ahead of the game and already have quotes, brochures, information to hand so you can give a rough idea of expenditure seemingly off the top of your head. Looks good and keeps you one step ahead of the rest.

promotional material is also pretty fixed. That leaves travel and staff meals/refreshments. No, you can't haggle with the rail companies or Shell Oil over the cost of petrol. That leaves the cost of feeding your team. £800 for three days – seems a bit on the generous side – that's £200 each (including yourself) for three days. What are you going to be eating, caviar? And drinking champagne? I think not: you're there to work. You could cut this down to a total of £400 and not starve anyone. Good, you've saved a bit so let's do a final budget – the one your MD will probably want to see before you go.

Exhibition rental	£600
Sales material	£500
Staff exhibition allowance (including you)	£2400
Staff meals/refreshments	£400
Travel	£240
Exhibition organiser	£5500
Total	£9640

Good, you're in under budget and have a little to play with. Pat yourself on the back and get on with organising that exhibition.

The rules for a special budget almost always follow the same lines and now you should have no difficulty doing one – and doing it quickly, professionally and smart.

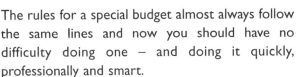

for next time

Always be ready for the special budget – they crop up quite often – and always ask what your budget is before agreeing to organise a project. Keep a good record of any expenditure over and beyond your normal departmental budget so you have something to refer back to – this is especially important when it comes to staff costs which can be complex to work out anew each time.

Be ready to delegate the task of organising a special event but retain control of the budget at all times. The budget is your most important tool and you should stay well in charge of it.

budget in an evening

Throughout this book we have assumed that you are under pressure – the pressure to produce a budget in a couple of days at most. But what if you really are under pressure? The pressure to produce a budget now, today – and you only have an evening to prepare? Well, it can be done. First, you'll need to have a copy of last year's budget. Go through it and check it against the actual figures for what really happened last year.

Now sit down and work out exactly what staff you have and what staff you need. Use the equation on page 72 to calculate your payroll percentage. Add this on to your basic payroll budget. You should know what you are paying your staff as a basic salary. From last year's figures you can see the actual amount. Calculate the total you will need to find to pay the staff everything including NI, pensions, cars and bonuses. This is the biggest single expenditure and the one that probably accounts for around 50 per cent of your budgeted total. Get this one right and you are more than half way.

Don't worry at this stage about a monthly breakdown. Work only with total figures for the year. Look at the actual figures for last year. What was your next biggest expenditure? Is this going to be around the same or more this year? Why? Check the next two biggest expenditures and by now you should be around 80 per cent of your budgeted total. The rest should now slot in, leaving you room to manoeuvre.

Now you can divide everything by 12 to give you a monthly figure. It won't be very accurate but at least you have some sort of figure to enter. You won't have any seasonal differences but that can wait until you've more time.

That's about it. There's little more you can do now. Buy more time by getting into your boss's office early and start firing questions. The more questions you ask, the fewer there will be for you to answer. Fight fire with fire. They've put you on the spot by asking for a budget in an evening. Now make them pay by putting them on the spot and demanding all the information you obviously haven't been given.

Someone, somewhere isn't doing their job properly. Make sure it isn't you.

Someone, somewhere isn't doing their job properly. Make sure it isn't you

budget in an hour

O K, so a budget in an evening isn't enough of a challenge for you. How about a budget in an hour? It has happened. What do you do if it happens to you? Well, apart from burning your budget and claiming it was an act of God …

You have an hour. Quickly now:

1 Get last year's budget.

2 Do a quick check to make sure there is nothing there that shouldn't now be. Make sure there is nothing missing that you've now got to account for.

3 Do a quick check that your staffing levels are about similar.

4 Run through the figures and add 15 per cent on to all of them.

5 Fill in as much as you can.

6 Take one or two items and make a note about them – any note, it doesn't matter. You now have a budget which looks about right.

That's all you can hope for in an hour.

This temporary budget should buy you enough time to do a real one. Let's hope so.